Managing
your
Money

Expert advice from:

Stephanie Fitzgerald
Head of Young People Programmes
The Money Charity
https://themoneycharity.org.uk

Ron Cirillo
Senior Leader, Financial Information Services,
Thomson Reuters, US and UK

Martina Collett
Careers and Employability Officer
South Thames College, London

USBORNE
Managing your Money

JANE BINGHAM
AND HOLLY BATHIE

Designed by Vickie Robinson
and Stephanie Jeffries

Illustrated by Nancy Leschnikoff
and Freya Harrison

Edited by Felicity Brooks
and Carrie Armstrong

USBORNE QUICKLINKS

The internet is a great source of financial information, but it's very important to know which sites you can trust.

We have selected some useful websites to supplement the information in this book and these are available at Usborne Quicklinks. Here you can find helpful tips on saving money and being a smart shopper, as well as fun activities to help you practice your money-managing skills.

For links to all these sites, go to:

www.usborne.com/quicklinks

and enter the keywords "managing your money."

When using the internet, please follow the internet safety guidelines shown on the Usborne Quicklinks website. Children should be supervised while using the internet.

INTRODUCTION

This book is designed to help you take charge of
your finances and make the most of your money.
It's full of tips on how to earn money, how to be
a smart spender, and how to plan ahead, so you can
spend your money on the things and people that
really matter to you.

You'll learn how to make a budget, manage your
expenses, and set aside money for giving and saving.
You'll also look ahead to the kinds of financial choices
you'll be making in the future.

The money habits you develop when you're young
usually stay with you for life. So now's the
time to start managing your money!

CONTENTS

1. HOW DO <u>YOU</u> MANAGE YOUR MONEY?   9

2. SO, WHAT IS MONEY?   13

3. THINKING ABOUT YOUR MONEY   20

4. SETTING UP A BUDGET   34

5. EARNING MONEY   40

6. SMART SPENDING   53

7. BUYING AND SELLING ONLINE   68

8. PHONES, GAMES, AND APPS   72

9. RETURNS AND REFUNDS   82

10. HAVING FUN   88

11. GIVING PRESENTS   93

12. GIVING TO CHARITY   96

13. STARTING TO SAVE   100

14. BANKS AND YOU   110

15. WORK AND PAY   124

16. STUDENT FINANCES   133

17. PAYING BILLS   138

18. RENTING AND MORTGAGES   142

19. BORROWING MONEY   147

20. GAMBLING   159

21. INVESTING   161

22. INSURANCE   166

FINDING HELP AND ADVICE   175

MONEY WORDS AND TERMS   177

INDEX   196

HOW DO <u>YOU</u> MANAGE YOUR MONEY?

Are you confident that you're in charge of your finances, or do you feel you don't always make the most of your money?

Try the quick quiz on the next two pages to find out more about your money habits. Be as honest as you can, and don't worry about giving the "right" answer. Learning to manage your money can take time and practice, but it's a skill that anyone can learn.

You could do the quiz again once you've finished the book, to see how much you've learned.

Quick Quiz

1. Do you always keep track of how much money you have?

A. No. I just spend my money, and stop when it runs out.

B. Sort of. I have a rough idea of how much money I have.

C. Yes. I keep a record of my money and my spending.

2. Do you ever find yourself running out of money?

A. Yes. I sometimes have to borrow from family or friends.

B. Almost never. I try to plan my spending.

C. Never. I always keep some money for emergencies.

3. Do you save up money for something special?

A. No. I'm hopeless at saving money.

B. Sometimes. But I often give up and spend the money instead.

C. Yes. I set aside a certain amount each week until I've reached my savings target.

4. You've been given a large gift of money. Do you . . .

A. Carry it with you in case you see something

you want to buy.

B. Keep it in a safe place at home.

C. Put it in a bank account* where it can gain

interest and grow.

* You can read about bank accounts in Chapter 14.

5. You've spotted an amazing pair of shoes. Do you . . .

A. Buy them right away — you can't wait to make

them yours.

B. Check if you can buy them at a cheaper price

before you make your move.

C. Give yourself some thinking time. You might decide

to spend your money on something else.

Answers

Mostly "A" answers?

You've got a way to go before you're a money expert. But don't worry, you've just begun your journey.

Mostly "B" answers?

You're usually sensible about money, but there are many useful skills you can discover.

Mostly "C" answers?

You're already careful with money, but you can still learn from this book.

SO, WHAT IS MONEY?

When you think of money, what do you see?
Do you picture a pile of coins and bills? Or maybe
you think of something invisible, that can be sent
over the internet with a simple click?

Money has changed many times over the centuries,
and it's changing now faster than ever. So, how did
we get to where we are today? Here's a quick tour
through the history of money, from ancient times
to the present day ...

EXCHANGING GOODS

For thousands of years, people didn't use money. Instead,
if they needed something (such as a camel), they found
something to exchange for it (such as some goats).

3 for 1!
It's a bargain!

SHELLS, BEANS, AND BEADS

Around three thousand years ago,
some traders had a bright idea. Instead of
exchanging actual things, they began using objects
to represent trading goods. Cowrie shells were used
in India and Africa. The Aztecs of Central Mexico
traded with cocoa beans, and some Native Americans
used colored beads, called "wampum."

METAL COINS

Metal coins were first used in Turkey around
the year 600BC. Later, the Ancient Greeks and
Romans each made their own set of coins, known
as a currency. Roman coins were stamped with the
head of the Emperor to show they were a currency
that could be trusted. Gradually, countries all over
the world developed their
own currencies.

PAPER MONEY

The first paper money was introduced in China in the 700s, but it was nearly a thousand years later that people in Europe began to print bills. In Europe, bills followed the creation of banks.

A bill is a promise from a bank to pay the amount printed on it.

CHECKS

In the 1700s, people started writing personal checks. A check is a promise to transfer money from one bank account to another. Checks were widely used until the end of the 20th century.

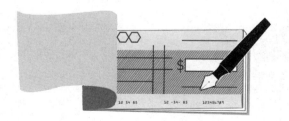

BANKCARDS

In the mid 1960s, a new way
of transferring money was
introduced. This was a plastic card
that could be recognized by a machine reader.
Bankcards are very useful for making payments,
and for taking money out of a bank account
using an ATM.

ONLINE PAYMENTS

By the 1990s, many people were paying for goods
online simply by typing the details of their bankcard
into a computer. This resulted in an automatic
transfer of money from buyer to seller. Online
payments led to the
rapid growth of online
selling companies.

TAP AND GO PAYMENTS

Around 2010, tap and go payments were introduced in many countries. This technology allowed people to make an instant payment simply by holding a bankcard or a smartphone close to a machine reader. Tap and go payments are not permitted for large sums of money.

THINK BEFORE YOU PAY

Paying by card is very quick and easy, but before you make a payment always make sure you check the amount carefully. Even though you're not counting out coins and bills, it's still important to ask yourself:

Do I REALLY have enough money to pay for this?

WHAT NEXT?

In the future, we may stop using cash altogether. Each time you make a payment, biometric scanners may recognize your face, your thumbprint, or your voice, and transfer your money automatically.

The way we shop today is changing rapidly, with many people doing most of their spending online. In the future, you may even use a personal shopping robot that's programmed to suggest what you should buy, based on your past spending habits.

BITCOIN — THE MONEY OF THE FUTURE?

In 2009, a new form of currency, known as "bitcoin," was created. Bitcoin is a virtual currency (or cryptocurrency) that doesn't exist as coins or bills, but can be used on certain sites online. People pay for goods or services using bitcoins stored in an online wallet.

It's hard to predict if bitcoin will survive, but some people believe that we will all be using some form of cryptocurrency in the future.

3.

THINKING ABOUT YOUR MONEY

A good way to start thinking about your money
is to ask yourself two simple questions.

- How much money do I have available to spend?
- How much money did I spend last week?

If you're struggling to answer these questions, you're
certainly not alone. But being vague about money can
make you feel uneasy. It can also lead to some
awkward situations when you discover
you've run out of cash.

I was sure I had some money somewhere.

Fortunately, it's possible to take some simple steps to keep on top of your spending, and the best place to start is with a money journal.

KEEPING A MONEY JOURNAL

Keeping a money journal will show you exactly how much money you have available to spend and how much you've paid out. Once you've gathered this useful information, you can start to plan ahead.

But first you need to choose the best way to keep your records ...

- You could use a notebook to jot down your spending.
- You could set up a money journal on a laptop, smartphone, or tablet.
- You could download a budget sheet to keep track of your expenses. You can find more money management advice on Usborne Quicklinks (see page 4).

MONEY IN AND MONEY OUT

Your money journal will show your money coming in (known as **income**) and your money going out (known as **spending**).

To keep a record of money in, note down all the amounts you receive and where they come from. At the end of each week, add up your weekly total.

To keep a record of money out, note down each time you pay for something. Add up the total at the end of each day and keep a weekly total, too. That way, you can compare your spending from day to day and week to week.

KEEPING RECEIPTS

It isn't always easy to note down all your spending, but if you keep receipts these will show you exactly how much you've spent. Try to get into the habit of adding up your "money out" at the end of each day. That way, you'll notice right away if you've spent too much.

WHERE DOES YOUR MONEY COME FROM?

Once you've set up a record of your money
coming in, you can start to think about where
it comes from.

REGULAR MONEY

You may receive a weekly or monthly allowance.
Or you may earn regular sums of money in payment
for jobs. These are all amounts that you can rely on
when you're planning your spending.

So, how much regular
money do I have available
to spend each week?

ABOUT ALLOWANCES

In any group of friends, there will always be some who have more spending money than others. But, whatever the size of your allowance, your challenge is to make your money work for YOU.

RANDOM AMOUNTS

Some of your "money in" could be unexpected. Maybe a relative has given you some money or you've won a prize? These are welcome extras, but they're not regular income so you can't include them when you plan ahead.

THINKING ABOUT YOUR MONEY IN

You may feel happy with the amount you have available to spend. Or you may decide you'd like to boost your income by earning extra money. There are ideas for earning money in Chapter 5.

WHAT DO YOU USE YOUR ALLOWANCE FOR?

Many teenagers are expected to use their allowance to pay for some essentials, such as food or clothes. This is very good practice for adult life, but it's important to be completely clear about the things your money is meant to cover.

For example:

- Will you be paying for lunches or only for snacks?
- Will you be buying everyday clothes or just a few fun extras?

It's a good idea to agree on some guidelines to help avoid any awkward misunderstandings.

HOW DO YOU SPEND YOUR MONEY?

Once you've recorded your "money out" for a few weeks, you can start to think about your spending patterns. Here are some useful ways to look at what you've recorded.

• What kind of things have I spent my money on?
Try dividing your spending into different categories, such as food, clothes, and gifts. This will help you decide if you've got the balance right.

Next month, I'm going to spend much less on clothes.

• Are my purchases "needs" or "wants"?
Learning to tell the difference between a need and a want is a vital money-managing skill.
Find out more on page 29.

- **Have I been charged too much?**

Look through your records for high-priced items.

Then ask yourself, could I have gotten them cheaper?

(You can find tips on smart spending in Chapter 6.)

- **Does my spending vary from week to week?**

Try comparing your spending week by week.

You should be able to see at a glance if you've

been spending too much.

NEEDS AND WANTS — CAN YOU TELL THE DIFFERENCE?

Next time you get ready to spend your money, stop yourself and ask: Is this a **need** or a **want**?

Needs are essentials that you can't manage without, such as shampoo to replace one that's run out.

Wants are luxuries that you don't really need, such as a second pair of sneakers, in a different color from the ones you already have.

It's fine to spend some money on wants, but first make sure you have enough to cover all your needs.

Do I really need all this stuff?

Quick Quiz

Take a look at the purchases below.
Can you decide which could be <u>wants</u> and which
could be <u>needs</u>? (Answers are on page 195.)

DEODORANT

candy

MAGAZINE

MOVIE
TICKET

SANDWICHES

BANANA

perfume

lipstick

BUBBLEGUM

TOOTHPASTE

BUS
TICKET

SOCKS

MONEY IN AND MONEY OUT

Once you have a clear picture of your money "in"
and "out," you can compare the two. Add up the
weekly totals for your money in (income) and your
money out (spending), and put them side by side.
Then prepare to ask yourself some tough questions.
Looking at your money records, do you:

> a) Always make sure you have more money
>   coming in than going out, so you
>   have money to spare for an emergency.
> b) Sometimes struggle to keep a balance
>   between money "in" and "out."
> c) Sometimes find yourself spending
>   more than you have coming in.

If you answered (a), you can relax, but if you
answered (b) or (c), you still have a way to go before
you become an expert money manager.

Money "in" minus money "out" = money left over

Sam's Money Journal

MONEY IN

Hmmm . . . I'd really like some more money to spend.

Week 1

Allowance	$15

Total = $15

Week 2

Allowance	$15
Yard work	$5

Total = $20

That's looking better. It's great earning extra money!

Week 3

Allowance	$15
Gift from Grandma	$10
Dog walking	$5

Total = $30

This week, I've got more income than I had last week, so I've decided to save some money.

MONEY OUT

Oh no — I've spent more than my allowance!
(I owe Mom $2.)

Week 1

Muffin	$1.50	Ice cream	$2.00
Milkshake	$3.00	Popcorn	$3.00
Phone case	$7.50	Total =	$17.00

Week 2

Pay back Mom	$2.00	Movie ticket	$9.00
Hot chocolate	$2.00	Potato chips	$1.50
		Total =	$14.50

I've got more money to spend this week, but I've still been careful.

Week 3

Smoothie	$3.00		
Sandwich	$4.00	Birthday gift	$4.50
Magazine	$3.50	Total =	$15.00

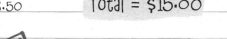

I'm saving up for headphones, so I've just spent my allowance this week and saved all the rest.

4

SETTING UP A BUDGET

Keeping a money journal will help you look back on your spending, but it's even more useful to plan your spending ahead. The best way to do this is to set up a budget. This will show you how much money you have coming in and will also help you plan your spending.

INCOME, EXPENSES, AND OTHER SPENDING

When you set up a weekly budget, the first thing you need to know is your **income** for the week.

Next, you need to note down all your **expenses**. These are payments that can't be avoided, such as travel costs to get to school, college, or work.

Once you've seen how much you need to spend on expenses, you can work out how much money you have left for **other spending.**

CREATING A BUDGET

One of the best ways to set up a budget is to create a simple spreadsheet on your computer, tablet, or smartphone. Spreadsheets have columns that you can use to show your income, your expenses, and your other spending. Using a simple spreadsheet will let you compare totals so you can see at a glance if you have enough income to cover your expenses, and how much money you have left for other spending.

BUDGETING HELP

Go to Usborne Quicklinks (see page 4) to download a budget sheet to keep track of your income and expenses.

MAKING A WEEKLY BUDGET

To make a simple weekly budget, you need two columns: one for **income** (money coming in) and one for **expenses** (money you need to set aside to spend on essentials).

When you subtract your expenses from your income, you can see how much money you have left, and plan your spending for the week ahead.

Take a look at Ethan's weekly budget, showing his income and his expenses.

Income		Expenses	
Allowance	$20.00	2 x lunches	$12.00
Pet-sitting	$5.00	Bus tickets	$3.00
Total	**$25.00**	**Total**	**$15.00**

I need to subtract my expenses from my income to see what I have left to spend.

$25
- $15
= $10

PLANNING YOUR SPENDING

Once you've calculated your spending money for the week, you can add a column to your budget for **other spending**. Make sure this total doesn't add up to more than you have left to spend.

Income		Expenses		Other spending	
Allowance	$20.00	2 x lunches	$12.00	Magazine	$3.50
Pet-sitting	$5.00	Bus tickets	$3.00	Snacks & drinks	$5.50
Total	**$25.00**	**Total**	**$15.00**	**Total**	**$9.00**

I need to stay inside my spending limit of $10.00, so I'm planning to spend $9.00 this week.

MONEY LEFT OVER

If you have money left over at the end of the week, you could add it to your income for the following week, or you could put it aside for savings.

See Chapter 13 for more on saving.

EXPANDING YOUR BUDGET

Budgets can be simple, like the one shown in this chapter, or they can have many extra columns. For example, you could add a column for your savings to your weekly budget.

WHO NEEDS A BUDGET?

Everyone, really. Companies and governments set up detailed budgets to plan how they'll spend their money and to make sure they don't overspend. Some families also use budgets to plan their household spending. You can make a budget for a week, a month, a year, or longer.

5

EARNING MONEY

There are many ways to earn money of your own. Take a look at the ideas on the next few pages and think about which ones could work for you.

PART-TIME JOBS

Once you reach the legal working age for your state, you may be able to find a part-time job in a store, business, or café. Ask local businesses about their hiring terms, as these will vary from store to store and state to state.

As well as providing regular money, a part-time job will give you valuable experience of the world of work and will equip you with some useful skills.

BEFORE YOU START A PART-TIME JOB . . .

- Check with your parents or guardians that they are happy for you to take on a regular job.
- Make sure you'll be able to travel to work easily, and that your new job won't interfere with school or other commitments.
- Ask for a written schedule with the days and times you're expected to work, and let your employer know well in advance about any dates you can't work.

JOBS AT HOME

Some parents are happy to pay for jobs around the house. Why not try suggesting some of the jobs on this page? (Don't be surprised if you're expected to clean up your room for free, though.)

 Dusting

 **WASHING THE CAR**

CLEANING OUT CLOSETS

VACUUMING

RAKING UP LEAVES

MOWING THE LAWN

WATERING PLANTS

JOBS FOR FRIENDS AND NEIGHBORS

Once you're confident that you have some useful
skills, you could offer to work for neighbors and
friends. Maybe you could mow your neighbors'
lawn or put out their trash cans? Or perhaps
you could feed their cat or water
their plants while they're
on vacation?

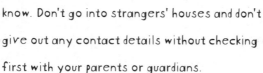

SAFETY FIRST

When you're working for
neighbors, stick to people you
know. Don't go into strangers' houses and don't
give out any contact details without checking
first with your parents or guardians.

WORKING WITH ANIMALS

If you're good with animals, you
could help friends and neighbors by ...

• Pet-sitting

This usually involves feeding a pet at regular times
and making sure it's happy and healthy.

• Cleaning up after animals

Some pet owners would be more than happy
to hand over the messy task of cleaning out
pet cages or kennels.

• Dog walking

This is a good job if you like walking,
but you'll need to be confident that
you can keep the dogs under control.

HELPING WITH CHILDREN

If you've taken a babysitting course, you could offer to babysit on weekends or evenings. Or, if you don't have much experience yet, you could help parents who work from home, by looking after their children while they get on with their work.

IT SUPPORT

Your IT skills could come in very useful if any of your friends or family need help getting to grips with technology. Maybe you could help them find their way around a smartphone or tablet, or help them to set up their computer?

PARTY ENTERTAINMENT

Are you good at juggling, magic tricks or face-painting? If so, you could help with children's parties.

When you're entertaining young children, it can be easier to work with someone else. You could get together with a friend to present a magic display or a puppet show, but you'll need plenty of practice first.

SHARING JOBS

When you share a job with friends, you have to share the money you make as well. Make sure you charge enough to make the job worthwhile for everyone. You can find advice on charging for your work on pages 48 to 51.

MAKING THINGS

Do you like designing and making things? And can you use your skills to make attractive items to sell? Here are just a few ideas to help you get started...

- You could sew, knit, or crochet hats, clothes, or toys.
- You could produce calendars or cards.
- You could create ornaments or jewelry.
- You could make an attractive bird feeder.

You'll find instructions for making things on Usborne Quicklinks (see page 4).

MAKING A PROFIT

When you decide on a price for something you've made, it's important to be sure that you can make a profit. A profit is the difference between the price of an item and the costs involved in making it.

Think about the money you've had to pay out so far. Maybe you've bought beads for making jewelry? Or maybe you've paid to print posters to advertise your sale? If you want to make a profit, your price will need to cover these costs.

We've worked out what to charge for our cards so we can make a profit.

You can see how we've calculated our price on pages 50 to 51.

YOUR TIME MATTERS TOO

If you were making a hand-made present for your grandma, she would really appreciate the time it took you to make her gift. But if you were earning money from selling hand-made goods, it would be important to add the cost of your time to what you charge. For example, if you were knitting hats, you would need to include a cost for your time as well as the cost of the yarn.

BE REALISTIC

Of course, you want to make a profit on the things you're selling, but when you're setting your prices, you'll need to be realistic, too. Look at the prices of similar things. You probably won't be able to charge much more.

AMIT AND AMY'S PLAN TO MAKE A PROFIT

This is the plan we made to sell our cards . . .

First, we decided how many
cards we wanted to make.

Let's make **100** cards.

Then we thought about what materials we would
need and how much they would cost.

Materials	Cost	Quantity	Totals
card stock	60¢ per sheet	10 sheets	$6.00
tissue paper	$5 per package	2 packages	$10.00
glue stick	$1 per stick	2 sticks	$2.00

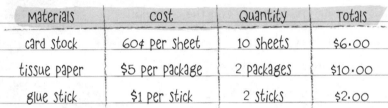

Total cost = $18.00

Next, we divided this total by the number of cards to find
the materials cost of one card.

$18.00 divided by 100 = 18¢

Each card will cost us
18¢ in materials.

But we still needed to add in the cost of our time . . .

First, we calculated the labor cost of each card.

> Let's say the labor cost of us both making cards is $10 an hour.

> Between us, it will take an hour to make 20 cards, so we need to divide $10 by 20.

$10 ÷ 20 = 50¢

> The labor cost is 50¢ for each card.

Then we added the materials cost to the labor cost to find the cost of making one card.

18¢ + 50¢ = 68¢

> Each card costs us 68¢ to make.

Using this information, we decided on a price per card that would cover all our costs AND make a profit.

> What would our profit be if we charged $1.50 a card?

$1.50 (price per card) minus 68p = 82¢

> We're making a profit of 82¢ on each card. So, how much would we make if we sold all 100 cards?

$0.82 (profit per card) × 100 = $82.00

> $82 is a good profit!

Quick Quiz

Can you work out how to make a profit?

(Answers are on page 195.)

a) If the cost of materials to make 12 hand puppets is $30, what is the cost of materials for each puppet?

Materials cost per puppet = _____

b) If you charge $8 per hour for your labor (work) and you make 4 puppets an hour, how much will it cost you to make each puppet?

Labor cost per puppet = _____

c) Can you calculate the total cost of making each puppet? (Total cost = materials cost + labor cost)

Total cost per puppet = _____

d) How much should you charge for each puppet if you want to make a profit of $1.50 per puppet?

Price per puppet = _____

SMART SPENDING

6

How do some people manage to make their money go so far, while others keep running out of funds? This chapter offers advice on how to be a smart spender and save money on:

- food and drinks
- clothes and shoes
- beauty and grooming products.

It also shows you how to make sense of discounts, price cuts, and special offers.

But, first, take a look at the spending tips on the next page.

THREE SMART SPENDING TIPS

1. SLOW DOWN

Before you spend any money, stop and ask yourself:
Do I really need this? Or do I just want it?

NEED?

WANT?

2. PLAN AHEAD

Think about what you need in advance and try to
avoid impulse buys. It's easy to make bad choices
when you're feeling rushed.

3. PLAY IT SAFE

Always keep your receipt and make sure you can
return your purchase if you need to. (You can read
about returns and refunds in Chapter 9.)

FOOD AND DRINKS

Food shopping is one of the biggest expenses that most teenagers face. Of course, it's important to eat plenty of healthy food, but there are some simple ways to cut down on your spending and still end up with healthy, tasty food.

Next time you go shopping for food, try these money-saving tips.

- **Compare prices for similar products.**
Take a few minutes to check the prices for different brands. You may be surprised to see how much they vary.

- **Look out for store-brand items.**
Store-brand products can be just as good as name brands, but they often cost less.

- **Check for reduced items.**

You'll usually find some items, such as bread from the bakery, have been reduced for a quick sale.

- **Look out for ads and coupons.**

Check the store's weekly ad before you shop to see if what you need is on sale, or download a coupon app.

- **If there's something you eat a lot, buy it in bulk.**

A multipack of snack bars is cheaper than the same number of individual bars and it should keep you going for several days.

BUY IN TIME

You can find bargains in the reduced section of most supermarkets, but if you're buying meat, fish, or dairy products, check their expiration dates and make sure you use them right away.

WHAT ABOUT SPECIAL OFFERS?

Special offers and discounts can be good money savers, but don't get drawn into buying something you don't need. Before you go for that tempting three-for-two offer, remember to ask yourself:

Why am I buying more than I really need?

STICK TO YOUR LIST

Do you sometimes arrive at the checkout with all sorts of things you don't really need? If you write a grocery list and stick to it, it will help you avoid expensive impulse buys.

CALCULATING DISCOUNTS

Here is a quick way to calculate discounts that are shown as percentages. If you first work out 10% (ten percent) of the original price, you can use this amount to calculate other percentages.

You can calculate 10% of the original price by dividing the price by 10.

The discounted price is
$15 minus $1.50 discount = $13.50

Now you know that 10% of the original price is $1.50, you can use this figure to work out other discounts.

A discount of 20% is 10% x 2.

The discounted price is

$15 minus $3 discount = $12

A discount of 40% is 10% x 4.

The discounted price is

$15 minus $6 discount = $9

DISCOUNTS AT A GLANCE

Many people find it easier to think in fractions, such

as halves and quarters, rather than percentages.

Here's a quick guide to some common discounts:

50% off = 1/2 price

33% off = 1/3 (a third) off

25% off = 1/4 (a quarter) off

75% off = 3/4 (three quarters) off

WHAT'S THE BEST VALUE?

It can be hard to tell if you're getting value for money when food comes in so many different packages. Fortunately, there is often a quick and easy way to compare prices.

How can I tell which one is the best value for money?

?

Many stores selling food and drinks show the unit price of the goods on sale. This is the cost of goods per item or per measure (for example, per ounce or per gallon).

LOOK FOR THE UNIT PRICE

Look for the unit price at the bottom of the price label. This will allow you to compare the cost of items, even when they're packaged in very different ways.

Orange juice (½ gallon)

$3.00

$6/gallon

Orange juice (1 gallon)

$5.50

$5.50/gallon

This is the best value.

Bag of oranges (5 pack)

$3.50

$0.70 each

Oranges (loose)

$0.75

$0.75 each

It's cheaper to buy the bag of oranges rather than five loose oranges.

BUYING CLOTHES AND SHOES

Shopping for clothes and shoes can be a lot of fun,
but it's all too easy to make expensive mistakes.
Next time you're tempted to pay out lots of money,
ask yourself these questions.

• Does it really fit ?

Is it too big or too small? Does it feel uncomfortable?

• When will I wear it?

Do you really want to spend a lot of money on
something you'll only wear a few times?

• Is it hard to keep clean?

Clothes that are "dry clean only" work
out to be very expensive in the long run.

• Do I have something almost the same at home?

Is it a want or a need? (Turn back to page 29
to remind yourself about wants and needs.)

If you still feel happy with your choice,
it's time for the next big question.

Am I paying too much?

This is when you need to do some checking . . .

If you're out shopping, check out other stores
to see if you can find something cheaper. You can also
check online to see if you can buy the same item at a
cheaper price.

If you're shopping online, search other sites for
special offers or sales.

Once you've done your research, you may choose
to go ahead — confident that you're getting a good
deal. Or you may decide to hold back for a while.
This will give you time to look around some more, or
to wait for a sale when you can find some bargains.

PRELOVED CLOTHES

You can find some amazing bargains in second-hand shops or on selling sites online. Often, clothes and shoes that have never even been worn are sold at a fraction of their original cost.

Thrift stores are excellent places to look for interesting clothes. And if they are run by a charity, you'll be giving to a good cause, as well as saving money.

Some people create a distinctive style by putting together vintage items from thrift stores. Even if you don't buy a whole outfit, you might like to buy a few retro items.

RETRO BARGAINS

TOILETRIES AND BEAUTY PRODUCTS

Of course you want to look — and smell — your best, but before you blow your cash on the latest "magic formula," take a look at the advice below.

- Try before you buy. Ask for a tester sample to try, and only buy products that you're sure are right for you.

- Don't let glamorous ads push you into buying top-price items. Check out beauty and grooming blogs for lower-cost options.

- Test out moisturizers and fragrances on your skin and wait a while before you hand over your money. You may have an allergic reaction to some products.

- Hold a party with your friends, and trade the products that don't work for you.

IT'S OK TO MAKE MISTAKES

Don't get too demoralized if you feel you've wasted your money. Everyone makes shopping mistakes sometimes. Think of them as useful experiences in your progress to becoming a smart spender.

Can you spot a bargain, or do you get confused by special offers? Take a look at these offers and decide which is the best deal in each pair. (Answers are on page 195.)

a) 2 FOR 1   OR   b) SECOND ITEM 1/2 PRICE

c) 2/3 ORIGINAL PRICE   OR   d) 20% off

e) half price   OR   f) 60% OFF

Can you work out the new, discounted, price of the clothes below?

SHORTS $20 NOW 25% OFF

T-SHIRT $12 NOW 1/3 OFF

7.

BUYING AND SELLING ONLINE

Online shopping is a good way to compare prices, find bargains, and save yourself money, but it can come with risks. So, how can you protect yourself online and enjoy shopping in safety?

BE A SAFE SHOPPER

Make sure your parents know about what you are planning to buy online. If you follow the guidelines below, they will also help to keep you protected.

- Always use a secure internet connection for your online shopping so your financial details can't be stolen.

- Avoid public Wi-Fi sites, such as in cafés or shopping centers, where other users could access your information.

- Check that the seller's website is secure. Look out for a padlock symbol in the address bar next to the website address. If you click on this symbol and a warning comes up, leave the site.

- Take a careful look at the seller's return policy. (You can find out more about returns in Chapter 9.) Sites with no information on returns should be avoided.

- Choose strong passwords for your online accounts, using a combination of upper and lower case letters and numbers.

- If you're asked if you want to "save" your card details, always play it safe and click "no."

- And finally — be suspicious! If a deal seems too good to be true, it probably is.

ONLINE AUCTIONS — THINK BEFORE YOU BID

Online auctions can be exciting, but you need to be careful not to get carried away. You can end up spending much more than you'd planned and then there's no going back. If your bid is successful, you will be committed to buying an item and you might not have the right to return it.

ONLINE SELLING

Online selling can be a good way to clear out your clutter and make money, but it's very important to stick to some basic safety rules.

- Never contact buyers or sellers yourself. Ask a parent or guardian to do it for you.
- Make sure you don't appear in any photos of items for sale.
- Always follow the safety guidelines provided by selling sites.

You could also think about getting together with friends or family members to sell your unwanted clothes, books, and games in a group yard sale.

8

PHONES, GAMES, AND APPS

Your phone can be a major money guzzler. Charges can add up fast, and phones can be damaged, lost, or even stolen. Here are some ways to help cut your costs and keep your phone safe.

BUYING A PHONE

There will always be pressure to have the latest model, but buying something less flashy could be a smarter move. If you go for a less expensive phone:

- You won't feel so upset if you damage or lose it.
- It won't cost a fortune to replace.
- You'll have more money to spend on other things.

I'm so retro, I'm back in fashion.

LOOKING AFTER YOUR PHONE

- Always keep your phone in a safe place.
- Invest in a sturdy cover to protect it from bumps and drops.
- Make sure your phone is password protected — and don't choose a password that's easy to guess.
- NEVER keep important financial information, such as your bank PIN, on your phone.
- Consider insuring your phone, so you can cover the cost of replacing it. (Phones can usually be covered by a family's home contents insurance, see page 172.)

AND IF IT GOES MISSING . . .

- Let your parents or guardians know right away.
- Contact your service provider and report it missing.

PHONE CONTRACT OPTIONS

You need to be 18 to have your own cell phone contract, but if you are younger, it's still useful to know the choices available, to help your family choose the right one for you.

Cell phone contracts offer an allowance of texts and calls for a monthly charge. Most plans also include a data allowance for internet use.

There are many different plans, offering a range of allowances for calls, texts, and data. Many plans offer unlimited calls and texts, but other plans are limited. If you choose a limited plan, you will need to stay within your plan's allowance or your bill will increase.

Aim to choose a plan that fits the way you use your phone without being too expensive. It's also a good idea to choose a flexible plan that allows you to change to a different one if you realize it's better suited to your needs.

I check my usage at the end of each week.

DATA LIMITS

Some phone contracts come with a data limit. This means that once you've used up your month's data allowance, it is cut off until the end of the month. Some families choose this type of plan so that the bill-payer is never faced with unexpected charges.

BYOP (BRING YOUR OWN PHONE)

Many phone plans include the price of a phone, but with a BYOP contract you bring your own phone. The phone service company simply provides the SIM card to go inside your phone and charges you for the use of calls, texts, and data.

As well as being cheaper than most standard contracts, BYOP deals allow you to change your plan more easily.

PREPAID PHONES

One sure-fire way to make sure you don't overspend is to go for a prepaid "pay as you go" deal. You don't have to sign a contract, so you can have a prepaid phone at any age.

Anyone can have a prepaid phone!

With a prepaid deal, you have your own phone. You use a re-loadable card to make your payment to the phone service company in advance, and your phone stops working as soon as you've used up your money. A prepaid deal allows you to pay if and when you can afford it, and you can even decide not to use your phone for a while.

CUT YOUR PHONE COSTS

The most common reason for exceeding your plan allowance is excess data use. Here are some ways to cut down on data use on your smartphone.

- Connect to a local Wi-Fi source whenever you can, and turn off data roaming.
- Switch off any apps and games you're not using.
- Beware of data gobblers, such as movies, live-streamed videos, and TV programs.

GAMING

If you're into gaming, you can find yourself paying serious money. As well as the cost of the games, there are tempting ads for bigger and better consoles, keyboards, controllers, and headsets.

You can make a big difference to your costs if you decide NOT to buy everything new. You could set up a swap group with your friends, or look online for pre-owned games and sell your own unwanted games. That way, you'll be spending less and having more gaming fun.

WATCH OUT FOR HIDDEN COSTS

Many game apps that are free to download are designed to encourage you to spend money. Just as the game is getting exciting, a message will flash up on the screen, asking if you want to access more levels, win back lives, or buy new objects. If you're not very careful, you can find yourself pressing the "buy now" button, without even stopping to think about the cost. Turn the page to find out more about in-app charges.

 ## IN-APP CHARGES WARNING

Whenever customers register with an app store, they are asked for details of their bankcard. Each time the customer presses "buy" inside an app, the payment is charged automatically to their card. This can result in some serious charges, and there are stories of kids spending thousands of dollars on their parents' bankcards without even realizing they've paid real money.

Fortunately, there's a way to avoid unexpected in-app charges. If you register a prepaid card with a limited amount of money, you will never go beyond your payment limit. (See page 118 for more about prepaid cards.)

FREE TRIAL ALERT

Some apps that are free to download are actually subscriptions that can end up costing you money every month.

Watch out for apps with a free trial period. This usually lasts a month, and after that date you can find yourself facing monthly charges.

Remember to note the date when the free trial ends so you can cancel your subscription. Otherwise, payments will be taken automatically from your bankcard. Once you've started paying monthly subscription fees, you may face a cancellation charge when you try to stop them.

Give me more money NOW!

9.

RETURNS AND REFUNDS (PLAYING IT SAFE)

Even experienced shoppers sometimes make mistakes, especially when they're buying things online. You can end up with something that's faulty or damaged, the wrong size or color, or even completely different from what you'd expected. Luckily, this needn't mean you've wasted your money. As long as you follow the rules explained in this chapter, you will usually be able to return your purchase and get your money back.

CHECK BEFORE YOU BUY

Before you hand over your money, you need to make sure you won't be stuck with something you can't return.

- If you're in a store, ask a sales assistant about the return policy before you make your payment. Or you can look for a sign near the cash register.
- If you're shopping online, find the section labeled "Returns" and read it through carefully before confirming your order.
- Remember that some items, such as underwear and earrings, are almost always non-returnable.

CLEARANCE WARNING

When stores hold sales to clear out their old stock, there are special rules for returning clearance items. Often, there's only a short time allowed for returning a purchase, and some items can't be returned at all.

REMEMBER TO KEEP YOUR RECEIPT

If you want to return an item, you'll need to show your receipt as proof of purchase. Some stores provide e-receipts, but many still use paper receipts. Stores usually have a time limit for returns, such as 30 or 90 days, so try to get into the habit of keeping your paper receipts in a special place, such as a shoebox, so you know exactly where to find them.

If you've lost your receipt, the seller may still take back the unwanted item, but instead of a refund you may be given a gift card or store credit to spend in their store.

I wish I'd kept my receipt somewhere safe.

REFUNDS AND STORE CREDIT

A refund is a repayment of the exact sum that you paid. You are entitled to a refund if an item is faulty and you have proof of purchase, so long as you've followed the seller's return policy (see page 86).

If you've lost your receipt, you may be offered some form of store credit. This may be a plastic card or a printed slip and it allows you to buy goods up to the value of the item you've returned. Usually, the credit can only be used in the store (or chain of stores) where you made your purchase and it may have a time limit.

LOOK AFTER YOUR STORE CREDIT

- Make sure you use it before the time limit or you'll end up losing all the money you spent.
- Keep it in a safe place. There's no way to claim your money back if you've lost it.

RETURNING YOUR PURCHASES

Sellers can insist on certain terms before they agree to take back a purchase and refund your money.

• Always check the time limit for returning goods.

If you return your purchase after the time limit, the seller has the right to refuse a refund.

• Check any other terms and conditions.

Often these conditions state that an item must be returned in exactly the same condition as it left the seller, with the original packaging, tags, or labels. This means clothes or shoes mustn't show any signs of wear. If you wear your new shoes outside — even for just a few minutes — the soles will get dirty and you won't be allowed to return them.

You'll never get your money back on us.

- Items bought online and delivered to your home should be returned in the same packaging.

Even if you can't wait to see inside your package, open it carefully in case you need to send it back.

LOOKING AT A RECEIPT

This is the date of purchase. It proves you're returning your goods in the time allowed.

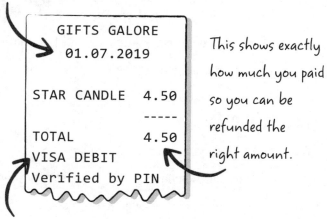

```
     GIFTS GALORE
      01.07.2019

STAR CANDLE   4.50
              -----
TOTAL         4.50
VISA DEBIT
Verified by PIN
```

This shows exactly how much you paid so you can be refunded the right amount.

This indicates that you paid by bankcard, so any money refunded will be put back into your bank account. If you originally paid in cash, you will be given a cash refund.

10

HAVING FUN

Having fun with friends can end up being very
expensive. So, how do you have a good
time without spending a fortune?

What to do...

IN OR OUT?

You don't always have to go out to have
a good time. Why not try planning some
"time in" with your friends? That way,
you'll save money, and your "time out" will feel more
special. Look at the page opposite for some ideas.

SETTING LIMITS

Sometimes you can end up spending a lot more on
going out than you'd planned. But if you get together
with friends to plan your outing, you can decide on
a spending limit in advance.

Once you know exactly how much you'll be
spending, you can relax and enjoy yourself, knowing
that your costs won't get out of hand.

FIVE MONEY-SAVING IDEAS
FOR FUN TIMES IN

1. Have a movie night at home. Make some popcorn, dim the lights and settle down to enjoy a movie.

2. Try living-room karaoke. Clear a space for a stage, and sing along to your favorite songs.

3. Organize a craft session and share your skills. Maybe you could turn what you make into money-saving gifts?

4. Hold a board game afternoon. (You can buy games cheaply in thrift stores.) Roll the dice, and start playing.

5. Hold a dance competition. Download some dancing tracks and try out some moves.

CUTTING COSTS

Often, the biggest expense when you're going out is the money you spend on food and drinks. With just a little planning, you can cut down on these costs.

I fill up my water bottle as I go. That way, I save money and help the environment.

I take homemade food to share with my friends.

I make my own smoothies. They save me lots of money!

I take my own hot drink rather than paying coffee shop prices.

We take our own food and drinks to baseball games when we can. Otherwise, our snacks can end up costing more than the tickets!

(Most baseball stadiums allow you to bring your own food and soft drinks.)

MEAL DEALS

If you decide you want to eat out, it pays to shop around for special deals. Look out for:

- Restaurants that offer early evening specials.
- Coupons from cafés and restaurants offering special deals. (But check the terms and conditions — some deals are not as good as they first seem.)
- Apps to help you track down the best value meals near you.

(Remember to check that the special offer or discount has been correctly applied to your bill.)

FIVE MONEY-SAVING IDEAS

FOR FUN TIMES OUT

1. Organize a ball game in the park.
2. Go on a bike ride with your friends.
3. Visit a free museum or gallery.
4. Search online for free events near you.
5. Look out for family coupons for

   special attractions.

GIVING PRESENTS

11

One of the most satisfying ways to use your money is to spend it on others. There's nothing like the feeling of giving a gift to someone you care about. So, how can you make the most of your money and give the kind of presents that show you care?

IT'S THE THOUGHT THAT COUNTS

You don't need to spend a fortune to make someone's day. Instead, you can use your time and talents to create something that's unique. Here are some ideas for gifts that will make the most of your money.

- Create a picture frame for a special photo.
- Decorate a jar and fill it with homemade cookies.
- Paint a flowerpot and plant some herbs in it.
- Make a calendar using your own photos.
- Bake and decorate a cake.

BIRTHDAY PROMISES

Do you sometimes have trouble thinking of the perfect present? Maybe you could promise a treat instead? Think of something special that the person you're treating would really enjoy. Then write out your promise in a card.

I promise to . . .

PUT ON A
SHOW FOR
YOU

BRING YOU
BREAKFAST
IN BED

Clean the house

WRITE YOU
A STORY

BUDGETING FOR PRESENTS

Are there times when you'd like to spend money on presents, but you find that you just don't have enough to spare? If so, you could look at building up a gift fund.

Once you've made a weekly budget for yourself, you can add a column for gifts. You could plan to save a regular amount each week, and, in the weeks before a busy present-buying time, you could increase the amount you set aside for gifts.

I usually set aside $5 a week for gifts.

Next month, I need to buy lots of presents, so I'm saving $10 a week.

12

GIVING TO CHARITY

When you give money to charity, you help make a difference — to other people's lives, to the environment, or to wildlife. It's good to know you're helping in some way and you don't have to be rich to be a charity champion.

- You can budget to make a donation to a cause you support.
- You can help some charities through your shopping choices.
- You can use your time and energy to raise money for a special cause.

I make cards and sell them for charity.

I buy Fairtrade products whenever I can.

RAISING MONEY

Raising money for charity is very rewarding — and it can be good fun, too. Why not get together with friends and plan what you can do to raise some funds?

FIVE IDEAS

FOR RAISING MONEY

1. Organize a car-wash team.
2. Put on a song and dance show.
3. Plan a sponsored run, swim, or sing.
4. Hold a bake sale.
5. Set up a face-painting stand.

GAINING SKILLS

When you raise money for charity, you're not just supporting an important cause. You're also gaining some valuable money-managing skills that will help you in your adult life.

FINDING SPONSORS

A good way to boost your charity funds is to find some sponsors. You could try approaching local stores or businesses, and asking them if they'd like to help.

- They may be willing to pay for some of your costs.
- They may donate food, equipment, or prizes.
- They may offer to match the money you raise.

In return for your sponsors' help, you can display their names as supporters of your event. Don't forget to include all the important information on a poster or flyer.

Name of event

Name of charity

Date, time, and place

Name of sponsor

MAY 3rd, 4PM, THE RECREATION CENTER

CHARITY DOG SHOW

All proceeds go to the
Puppy Protection League

LOTS OF EXCITING PRIZES!

SPONSORED BY
JUICY BONES

13. STARTING TO SAVE

Saving money makes you feel good. Once you start to put some money aside, you will find:

- You can start planning to buy the things you really want.
- You can save up money for gifts.
- You can keep some money in reserve to pay for unexpected expenses.

STARTING SMALL

Even if you've very little money to spare, it's still possible to start saving. Just decide on the amount you think you could put aside each week or month, and try to stick to it. Be realistic about what you can save and don't give up. You'll find your savings soon start adding up.

A SAVINGS EXPERIMENT

At the end of each day, check your pockets or wallet for any spare small coins and drop them into a jar — you'll probably find you don't miss them at all. Do this for a month, then count up what you've saved. You could use the money to buy something special or you could add it to your savings.

MAKE A SAVINGS PLAN

Whatever you're saving for, it helps to have a plan. First, set yourself a savings target (the total amount you need to save). Then you can work out how much you need to save each week, and how long it will take you to reach your target.

Once you've decided on your target, there are two ways to make a savings plan.

1) You can decide how much you want to save each week and calculate how long it will take to reach your target amount.

> My savings target is $40. If I save $4 a week, it will take me 10 weeks to reach my target.

$$\begin{array}{r} \$4 \\ \times\ 10 \\ \hline = \$40 \end{array}$$

2) You can decide how long you want to save for and calculate how much you'll need to save each week.

I don't want to wait 10 weeks to save up $40, so I'm going to save $8 a week. Then I'll reach my target in 5 weeks.

$40
÷ 5
= $8

Reaching a savings target feels very satisfying. And once you've reached one target, you can do it again and again.

I'm so glad I saved up for a guitar.

ADDING SAVINGS TO YOUR BUDGET

You can use your weekly budget* to help you plan your savings.

Joe has made a budget for the week showing his income and expenses.

Income		Expenses	
Allowance	$20.00	Lunch x 2	$12.00
Pet-sitting	$8.00	Bus tickets	$4.00
Total	**$28.00**	**Total**	**$16.00**

Once I've spent $16 on expenses, I'll have $12 left for other spending.

$28
- $16
= $12

Income	Expenses	Spending money
$28.00	$16.00	$12.00

* Turn back to page 36 to remind yourself about weekly budgets.

If I allow myself $7 for spending money, that will leave $5 for saving.

$12
− $7
= $5

Income	Expenses	Spending money	Savings
$28.00	$16.00	$7.00	$5.00

If I save $5 for the next 12 weeks, I will have saved $60. Then I'll have enough to buy the shoes I want.

$5
× 12
= $60

MONEY IN RESERVE

As well as saving up for something special, it's good to have some money in reserve. This is money you can use for emergencies — maybe to repair a broken smartphone or to pay for a taxi if you've missed your bus.

Having money in reserve can also give you the freedom to act on impulse and spend some money on something just because it feels right.

When you're planning your budget, you can set aside some money each month for your reserve fund. Or you may simply choose to top up your reserve fund when it's running low.

BOOST YOUR SAVINGS

It's good to get into the habit of boosting your savings. If you have unspent money at the end of a week, consider adding it to your savings fund. And if you're given money as a present, you could put at least some of it into your savings.

TIME FOR A BANK ACCOUNT?

If you're thinking about long-term saving, you might want to consider a savings account. You'll find more about banks in Chapter 14.

Quick Quiz

Can you make a savings plan?

(Answers are on page 195.)

a) If you could afford to save $6 a week for buying presents, how much money would you have saved up for presents after 5 weeks?

b) Suppose you have 8 weeks to save for a wetsuit costing $80. If you save the same amount every week, how much should you set aside each week?

c) Imagine you have a plan to save $20 a month towards a bike costing $200. Luckily, you've been given $40 in birthday money. If you add your birthday money to your savings, how long will it take you to reach your savings target?

BANKS AND YOU

There are some very good reasons why people choose to open a bank account.

- Banks keep your money safe.
- They keep a record of how much money you have in your account, showing money coming in and money going out.
- If you save money with a bank, the bank will add interest payments to your savings. (See page 119.)

LOOKING AT BANK ACCOUNTS

Banks offer two basic types of accounts for adults — a checking account and a savings account. **Checking accounts** are used for managing everyday money, for example receiving paychecks and paying bills. **Savings accounts** help people to save by keeping their savings separate from their other money, and by adding a small amount of interest to their savings.

Banks also offer accounts for under-18s, but these must always be held jointly with an adult.

- **Joint checking accounts** are usually opened by a parent for their child. Under-18s can access the account's features with a parent's permission.
- Adults can set up a **youth savings account** for a child of any age. These accounts are often used to save money for children to use when they are older.

WHICH BANK?

Today, there are three main types of banks to choose from: traditional retail banks, credit unions, and online-only banks. They all offer the same basic services, but with slightly different terms and conditions. Choosing the right bank for you is a decision for you and your family to make.

JOINT CHECKING ACCOUNTS

Joint checking accounts can give young teens the chance to start managing their own money. So long as the adult account holder gives their permission, the young account holder will be able to make deposits (put money into the account) and make withdrawals (take money out of the account).

Who opens the account?

Most joint checking accounts for teenagers are opened by a parent or a legal guardian.

What's the age range?

The usual age range for a young joint account holder is 14 to 17. At the age of 18, the young account holder can become the sole owner of the account.

Who can pay into the account?

Anyone can make a deposit into a joint account. So, if you have a part-time job, your earnings could be deposited in your account.

Can I use online banking?

Online banking via a computer, tablet, or smartphone is usually available for joint checking accounts.

Do I get a bankcard?

Banks can vary on what they offer, and they may have age restrictions on using cards. But you can usually have a debit card once your family feels you are ready for it.

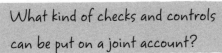

What kind of checks and controls can be put on a joint account?

Adult co-owners of a joint account can view any activity on the account. They may also choose to:

- Set up texts or emails to alert them to when the account is being used.
- Set a monthly limit on spending. Once the limit is reached, you won't be able to withdraw any money or use a bankcard for spending. Having a limit set on your account can be a very useful way to help you manage your spending, and stop you from using up all your money at once.

MORE ABOUT BANKCARDS

Checking accounts offer a debit card and a PIN (Personal Identification Number).

When account holders use their debit card, the money comes directly out of their bank account. You can use a debit card to withdraw cash, using an ATM, and to spend money in stores and online.

KEEP YOUR PIN SAFE

Your PIN should be a secret that only you know. Make sure you memorize it and never share it with friends.

TAKING OUT CASH

ATMs make taking out money simple and easy, but they need to be treated with care.

- Be careful when you're keying in your PIN. Always check that there's no one looking over your shoulder.
- Get into the habit of checking your balance (the amount of money in your account) before you withdraw any cash.

WATCH OUT FOR FEES

While some ATMs are free to use, many will charge you to withdraw your money. Check the charges before you withdraw any money and look out for ATMs offering free or low-cost withdrawals.

LOST CARD ALERT

If your card goes missing, you need to take action urgently. Call your bank to CANCEL your card, or ask a parent or guardian to call for you. An operator will block all payments and cash withdrawals so someone else can't use your card, and will arrange for a replacement card to be sent to you.

PREPAID BANKCARDS

An easy way to avoid overspending is to use a prepaid bankcard. If you use a prepaid card, you or your parents can decide exactly how much money to put on your card. Prepaid cards allow you to take out money and make payments. But when the money runs out, the card simply stops working until more money is added to it.

Prepaid cards are especially useful when you're traveling. It's much safer to carry a card than a wad of bills, and your parents may be able to add more money to your card for you to use in an emergency.

YOUTH SAVINGS ACCOUNTS

Youth savings accounts are co-owned by a young account holder and an adult "custodian." When the young account holder turns 18, their savings can be transferred to a regular savings account.

One advantage of keeping savings in a bank is the interest the bank will pay you. Interest is a percentage of your total savings that is added to your savings each year. So, the larger your savings amount, the more interest it will earn.

MORE ABOUT SAVINGS ACCOUNTS

The percentage of interest added to your savings each year is shown as an APY, or Annual Percentage Yield. This rate is used as a way of comparing different savings plans. The higher the APY, the more interest you will gain on your savings.

Interest rates on savings are much smaller than the interest rates that people are charged when they're paying back a loan. (These rates are known as APR and you can read about them on page 150.) This means you will only see a serious benefit for large savings (say over $1,000).

Youth savings accounts are often used by adults to deposit money for a child to use when they are older. Many parents choose to open an "education account," to save up money to pay for a child's college education.

ONLINE BANKING

Many people today manage
their bank account online.
With an online account, you can:

- Access your bank account from a computer,
  tablet, or smartphone.
- Check your bank balance any time you want.
- See exactly what's been paid in and what's
  gone out.
- Make payments to another person simply by
  typing the details of their bank account.
- Pay bills and set up regular payments.
  (See Chapter 17 for more on paying bills.)

SPECIAL FEATURES

Some online bank accounts are specially designed to make banking easier. They work on smartphones and tablets, and include such features as:

- Alerts to warn you when you're in danger of running out of money.
- Programs to help you save a certain amount each week.
- Systems to record your purchases in different categories, so you can review your spending patterns.

I find it really helpful to receive text alerts when my account is getting low.

ONLINE BANKING SAFETY

When you bank online, you need to take special care.

- Keep your login information strictly secret.
- Don't use the same password for your online banking as you do for other websites.
- Never use free Wi-Fi in cafés or stores to log in to your bank account, because other users may be able to access your personal details.

WATCH OUT FOR FRAUD

Some criminals try to gain access to bank accounts by sending a message by text, phone, or email. These messages appear to be from your bank and may request login details for your account, or ask you to type in your password. Don't reply. Ask a grown-up to check any message that seems suspicious and never give login details by phone or email.

15. WORK AND PAY

In the future, you'll find yourself facing all sorts of exciting new challenges. You may be starting a full-time job, joining an apprenticeship program, or beginning college, and all of these options will bring new money choices. This chapter covers work and pay, and the following chapter gives advice on student finances.

APPRENTICESHIP PROGRAMS

Employers in a range of industries run apprenticeship programs. These programs allow young people to combine work and study by mixing on-the-job training with classroom learning, either at a college or a training center. Apprentices are paid a wage while they gain valuable working skills and qualifications.

STARTING FULL-TIME WORK

Once you start full-time work, you will receive regular pay.

- **You may be paid a wage.**

Wages are payment for the hours you work, using a set hourly rate. Wages are most often paid every other week, but some employers may pay wages daily, weekly, or monthly.

- **You may get a salary.**

Employees on a salary receive fixed regular payments for their work. Salaries are usually paid directly into an employee's bank account on either a weekly, biweekly, or monthly basis.

Not everyone is paid wages or a salary. You can see some other kinds of payments on page 129.

WHAT'S THE MINIMUM WAGE?

In many countries, the government sets a minimum rate of pay per hour, and it is illegal for employers to pay under that sum. In the US, the national (or federal) minimum wage applies to all workers. Some states also set minimum pay standards above what is required by the federal government.

LOOKING AT SALARIES

Salaries are shown as the amount you earn each year. But this isn't the same as the pay you take home. A salary is the amount you earn before income tax and other charges are taken off.

Turn to page 130 to find out more about pay.

My annual salary is $40,000, but my take-home pay is $32,956 a year and I'm paid $2,746 a month.

HOW MANY HOURS?

In the US, the usual number of working hours for a full-time worker is 40 per week. However, some workers, such as doctors, are expected to work for many more hours than this. Your working hours are agreed directly with your employer, and may be formalized in a contract, depending on the type of work you do.

SEASONAL JOBS

Many jobs have working hours that vary according to the time of year. For example, a waitress in a seaside café may have to work for 40 hours, or more, a week in summer, but have very few hours' work a week in winter. People with seasonal jobs need to be very smart about budgeting to make sure they don't run out of money.

WHAT ABOUT OVERTIME?

When you do overtime, you work for longer
than the hours agreed with your employer, or for
longer than the hours governed by federal, state,
or local law. In some jobs, you may be paid extra
for working overtime, but this doesn't always
happen. It is very important, when you start a
new job, to discuss overtime with your employer
so you know exactly what to expect.

Some employees
aren't paid extra
for overtime. Instead,
they can take time off
to make up for any overtime
hours that they've worked.
This is sometimes known as
"comp time," which is short
for "compensatory time."

I'm working
late tonight.

ALL KINDS OF WORK

People can be paid for their work in a range
of ways. Here are some examples.

I'm a freelance designer. I charge
an hourly rate for my work.

I run my own business. I pay myself a
salary from the profits of my business,
and I pay my employees' salaries too.

I'm a picture framer. I have a set
of prices that I charge my customers.

I sell cars. As well as my salary,
I earn extra payment, known as
commission, on every car I sell.

LOOKING AT A PAY STUB

A pay stub doesn't simply show money earned. It also shows deductions — money **taken off** your earnings by the government and other organizations.

Looking at a pay stub you will usually see:

- Your gross monthly pay.
  This is your pay <u>before</u> any deductions.
- Your net monthly pay.
  This is your pay <u>after</u> deductions.

You will also see some or all of the items below:

- Your federal income tax payment.
- Your state income tax payment.
- Your health insurance payment, if you are enrolled in your employer's health insurance program.
- Your workplace pension contribution, if you are enrolled in a workplace pension plan.

WHAT IS INCOME TAX?

Income tax is a proportion of people's earnings that goes to the government to pay for public services, such as roads, schools, and the police.

Income tax is deducted from pay, but at the end of the year tax payers file a tax "return." If it turns out that they should have paid less in taxes (for example, because they are on a low income), the tax that was deducted from their pay is refunded to them.

Because income tax is in proportion to what you earn, people earning a large amount of money pay more in taxes than people with smaller incomes.

WHAT IS HEALTH INSURANCE?

For full-time employees, health insurance is usually part of their employee benefits. Employees pay a percentage of their income into a health insurance program, and their employer makes a contribution, too. Health insurance helps to cover the cost of medical expenses if you are sick or have an accident.

SAVING FOR RETIREMENT

Many employers offer a retirement savings plan, and the most common one is called a 401-k. Employees who join a 401-k plan pay a percentage of their income into an investment fund, and their employer often matches their contribution. The money in the investment fund gains interest over time. (You can read about investment on page 161.)

When employees reach retirement age, they can use their pension (the money they have saved, plus the interest it has gained) to provide an income for their later years.

Saving up for retirement doesn't seem remotely urgent when you're young, but it makes very good sense to start saving early. If you put it off until later, you'll need to make much larger payments just to save the same amount.

This is the life!

STUDENT FINANCES

16

If you decide to go to college, you may need to borrow money to help cover your costs. Student loans can be used to pay for the costs of a university course and for living expenses while you are studying.

There are many options for student borrowers, but most take advantage of the Federal Direct Student Loan Program. This program offers loans to college students. The amount that you can borrow depends on the cost of attending your college minus the contribution that your parents or guardians are expected to make, depending on their income.

Student borrowers have to pay back the money they have borrowed plus the interest payments that have been added to their loan. (See pages 149–151 to read about interest payments on loans.)

SUBSIDIZED AND UNSUBSIDIZED LOANS

Students may be offered a subsidized or an unsubsidized loan.

- If you have a subsidized loan, you won't pay any interest on your loan until you start making repayments.
- If you have an unsubsidized loan, interest will start being added to your loan right away.

Always choose a subsidized loan if you can, as you will end up paying back a smaller amount.

PAYING BACK STUDENT LOANS

If you have a subsidized loan, you won't usually start repaying it until six months after you graduate or leave school. (You will also need to start repaying your loan if your college hours drop below half-time.)

There are several options for making repayments.

- You can pay a set amount each month, based on paying back your loan within ten years.
- You may choose a graduated payment plan, in which payments start small, but become larger as your income grows.
- You may join an income-based repayment plan, in which you pay a percentage of your income, so the more you earn the more you pay.
- Some borrowers choose to repay their loans over a longer period than ten years. But this ends up costing them a lot more, as interest is added to every payment.

Now I'm earning more, I can make bigger repayments and pay off my loan faster.

EXTRA FINANCIAL AID

There are several extra sources of finance,
in addition to student loans, that can help
students to fund a college education.

- Grants provide financial help for students from
  low income households. They are usually one-off
  sums of money and they do not need to be repaid.

- Scholarships are awarded to promising students.
  Scholarship money is often used to pay the
  tuition fees for a course.

- The Federal Work-Study Program allows some
  students to earn money while they are studying.
  Students qualify for the
  program depending on
  their financial need.

STAR ACADEMY

PART-TIME JOBS

Some students take on part-time work
or find a job during school breaks. These
extra earnings can help to cover the cost
of student life, but combining study
with work can be a challenge.

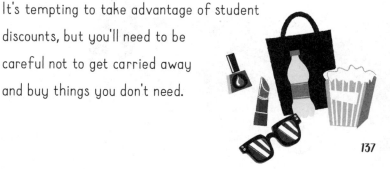

STUDENT DISCOUNTS

Some stores, gyms, and movie theaters offer
discounted student rates. There are also a few
travel sites that offer reductions for students.
It's tempting to take advantage of student
discounts, but you'll need to be
careful not to get carried away
and buy things you don't need.

17

PAYING BILLS

As you get older, you'll find you have lots of bills to pay. As well as household bills for services such as electricity, gas, and water, there may be phone bills, insurance, subscription payments — and more.

So, how do you stay on top of your bills and make sure they all get paid on time?
The most important thing is
to get organized . . .

TOP TIPS
FOR MANAGING BILLS

- As soon as you get a bill, check it carefully.
  If you spot a problem early, you'll have more
  time to sort it out before it's time to pay up.

- Note the "payment due" date and give yourself
  a reminder to pay well in advance.
  Highlight payment dates on your calendar
  or set up alerts on your phone.

- Store your bills in a safe place.
  If your bills are digital, you could set up
  a folder on your computer.

- Set up a payment system that works for you.
  Many people choose to pay their bills by direct
  debit. Turn the page to find out more.

PAYING BY DIRECT DEBIT

Once you've turned 18, you can set up direct debits through your bank, which will allow a company or an organization to take money out of your bank account on agreed dates. Once you've set up a direct debit, money is taken automatically from your bank account on the date your bill is due.

If you pay by direct debit, you'll never miss a payment and you'll never be late with your payments. But you will need to keep a careful check on your bank account to see what money has been taken out and when.

ELECTRICITY

MAGAZINE SUBSCRIPTION

WATER

Phone

INSURANCE

DIRECT DEBITS OR RECURRING PAYMENTS?

Direct debits and recurring payments are both methods of making automatic payments from a bank account, but they work in different ways and are used for different kinds of payments.

- For a **direct debit**, the amount leaving your account is decided by the company you're paying. So, the amount might change from month to month depending on the size of your bill. Direct debits are used for paying monthly bills, or rent payments.

- For a **recurring payment**, the amount leaving your account is decided by you, and the amount won't alter unless you change it. This method is used for regular payments that usually don't change, such as for annual subscriptions or monthy donations to charity.

18

RENTING AND MORTGAGES

Sometime in the future, you may start making plans to move into a rented apartment or house. And looking further ahead, you may even dream of buying a home of your own. This chapter covers some of the costs involved in renting and taking out a mortgage. It also provides a guide to the regular costs of running a home.

GETTING READY TO RENT

Moving into a house or apartment is an exciting step, but it comes with costs. Before you move in:

- You will be asked to pay your first month's rent in advance.
- You'll probably be asked to pay a security deposit (see page 144).
- You may need to pay a leasing agent's fee.
- If the place is unfurnished, you will need to buy furniture.

We need some chairs!

WHAT IS A SECURITY DEPOSIT?

A security deposit is a sum of money paid as a guarantee to cover the cost of possible damage to a rented property. The cost of a security deposit is usually about the same as one month's rent, and is kept until the tenants move out. It is returned in full if the landlord is satisfied that there is no damage.

BUYING YOUR OWN HOME

It's a wonderful dream to own your own home, but how do you go about it? Unless you're extremely wealthy, you'll need to take out a mortgage.

WHAT IS A MORTGAGE?

Most home-buyers have a repayment mortgage. This is a long-term loan from a bank or credit union that allows people to buy a house or a condo. The home-buyers repay the loan in monthly installments, with added interest payments (see page 149). Paying back a mortgage usually takes at least 30 years.

MAKING A DOWN PAYMENT

The first step towards taking out a mortgage is
to save up for a down payment. This is a chunk
of money that provides the first payment on a
property. In the US, a down payment is usually
20 percent of the purchase price, but there are
some offers for first-time
buyers that allow people
to buy homes with
a much smaller
down payment.

A LONG-TERM INVESTMENT

Because mortgage payments include added interest,
home-buyers end up paying a lot more for their
home than its original selling price. However, most
people think that having a mortgage is a good idea.
If you take out a mortgage instead of renting, your
payments are helping to pay for your own home,
rather than going into your landlord's bank account.

HOUSEHOLD EXPENSES

Once you are living in a place of your own, you'll need to think about your regular household expenses. These are some of the costs you'll need to budget for.

- Monthly rent or mortgage payments.
- Bills for gas, electricity, and water (unless they're included in your rent).
- Internet, phone, or cable bills.
- Home contents insurance.
- Bills for other services, such as trash collection, sewer services, etc.

It's a good idea to set up a household budget showing all your costs for the month. This will help you plan your spending to make sure you can always pay the rent and the bills.

BORROWING MONEY

Most people borrow money at some time in their lives.

- A couple may have arranged a line of credit with their bank to cover unexpected costs.
- A family may have a credit card that they use for booking vacations.
- Someone who is self-employed may take out a bank loan to help buy tools or a vehicle.

Borrowing money can be very useful in helping people to achieve their goals. But borrowers need to manage their loans carefully, to make sure they can pay back what they owe.

This chapter looks at different kinds of borrowing and the risks that they can bring with them.

LINES OF CREDIT

Once you have an over-18 checking account, you may be able to arrange a line of credit with your bank. This arrangement will allow you to withdraw extra money from your account up to an agreed limit. The money will need to be repaid within a certain time frame, and you will be charged interest on the amount you've borrowed until the loan is paid off.

 ## BEING OVERDRAWN

If you spend more money than you have in the bank, without first arranging a line of credit, your account will become overdrawn. Banks usually charge very high fees whenever an account is overdrawn.

It is very important to avoid being overdrawn. Always make sure you have enough money in your account to cover all your payments.

You owe the bank $25.

ADDING INTEREST

Have you ever borrowed money from someone you know? If so, you may have promised to pay it back within a certain time, but you probably didn't have to pay any extra charges.

Sadly, the world of loans doesn't work like this. When you borrow money from a bank or company, you agree to pay back the loan AND to pay interest on the amount you've borrowed. Interest is a percentage of the total sum you've borrowed and it can range in size enormously.

Oh no! I have to pay back my loan and pay the interest payments too!

LOOKING AT INTEREST RATES

The amount of interest you pay on a loan is shown as an APR, or Annual Percentage Rate. All lenders are required by law to show their APR, and this helps borrowers to compare interest rates. Credit cards have a much higher APR than bank loans and the APR on store cards is often even higher than on credit cards.

MAKING REPAYMENTS

Most repayments on loans are made in monthly installments with interest added to each payment you make. So, the longer you take to repay the loan, the more interest payments you will have to make, and the more money you'll end up paying.

TYPES OF BORROWING

There are many different ways to borrow,
but here are just a few.

• Bank loans

Banks offer loans to their customers, so long as
they are sure that the borrower can afford the
repayments. Banks charge lower interest rates
on repayments than most other lenders.

• Installment plans

Some sellers of expensive items, such as cars or
furniture, allow their customers to pay in monthly
installments plus interest. Customers can take away
their purchase right away, but paying back the loan
can take months or years, and end up costing
a lot more than the original price.

It took me five years to buy
my car and cost me $7,500
more than its original price.

- Credit cards

Credit card companies allow card users to borrow money up to an agreed limit. Card holders use their cards for spending, and pay back what they've borrowed in monthly installments.

CREDIT CARD REPAYMENTS

Credit card companies offer three monthly repayment options.

- You can pay back the full amount you owe.
- You can pay back part of what you owe.
- You can make the minimum payment.

If you repay the full amount on time, you won't be charged interest, but if you choose one of the other options you will have to pay interest on what you've borrowed, and it will keep adding up each month.

CREDIT CARD DANGER $ $ $

If you only make the minimum repayment each month, your repayments could drag on for years, with the amount that you have to pay back growing every month. A borrower could spend 30 years paying off a debt of $3,000, and end up paying many times the original debt because of all the interest that has added up.

• Store cards

Store cards can be used for shopping in a store or a chain of stores. They have lots of tempting special offers, but they usually have extremely high interest rates.

I thought my store card would save me money, but it's cost me a fortune!

CHANGING RATES

Some loans have a fixed interest rate, so borrowers know exactly how much interest they'll be paying each month, but many loans have a variable rate. This means borrowers need to keep checking to see how much interest they'll be paying.

Credit card and store card companies often offer a low interest rate as a way of encouraging people to borrow. But once a borrower starts using their card, interest rates can rise very sharply. Card holders should always check the APR on their monthly statement. If they are unhappy about the interest rate, they have the right to change to a different card.

I never imagined interest rates could rise so steeply.

PROBLEMS WITH REPAYMENTS

Borrowers who are late with their repayments on a loan or a card have to pay a fee, and possibly face an increased interest rate as well. And if they miss a payment or their payment is late, it will affect their credit score.

WHAT'S A CREDIT SCORE?

A credit score is a record of a borrower's repayments on loans and cards. When people apply to a lender for a loan or a mortgage, the lender checks their credit score before deciding whether or not to offer them the loan. (Credit scores are sometimes known as credit ratings.)

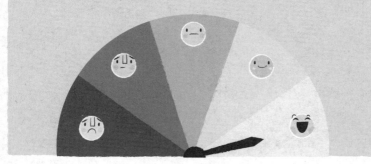

EMERGENCY BORROWING

People in financial difficulty may sometimes need a short-term loan just to keep them going until their next payday or until they can get a hold of some more money. "Payday" loan companies offer short-term loans, but they charge their borrowers very high repayment rates.

BEWARE OF LOAN SHARKS

Sometimes, people in need of money may turn to illegal lenders — often known as "loan sharks." These lenders may start off seeming friendly, but if a borrower falls behind with repayments, they can soon turn very nasty. Instead of sticking to a set interest rate, they raise their repayment rates whenever they wish, and may even use violence to get the money they want.

GETTING INTO DEBT

Once repayments start mounting up, people can find themselves struggling to pay back what they owe. It's all too easy to get caught in a vicious cycle, where borrowers need to borrow more in order to make their repayments.

Trying to keep up with loan repayments can feel like running as fast as you can, but still falling behind.

I can't seem to get anywhere however hard I run.

Fortunately, there are places where people can go to discuss their debt problems and get help with managing repayments. Go to Usborne Quicklinks (see page 4) for links to helpful websites.

FOUR GOLDEN RULES OF BORROWING

DON'T BORROW MORE THAN YOU HAVE TO

The bigger the loan you take out, the bigger the

repayments will be.

PAY THE MONEY BACK AS SOON AS YOU CAN

The longer you take to repay a loan, the more the

costs will add up.

MAKE SURE YOU HAVE A PLAN FOR REPAYING YOUR LOAN

Set aside enough money each month to make the repayments.

BE SURE NOT TO MISS A REPAYMENT

Missing a repayment will mean you have to pay extra fees

and can also affect your credit score (see page 155).

GAMBLING

20

When people gamble, they take risks with their money, even though they know that the chance of losing is much greater than the chance of winning.

Gambling can happen in a public place, such as a casino or a horse racing track. People can gamble at home and can access betting sites on the internet. Internet gambling is a very big business and many people gamble online in secret. Gambling is a high-risk activity, and for some people it can be dangerously addictive.

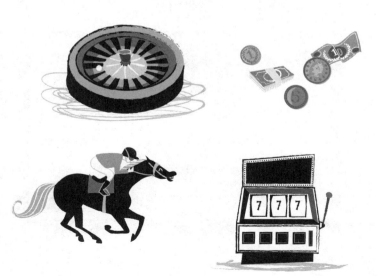

GAMBLING CAN START EARLY

Every state has laws that govern the minimum age for gambling, but there is still evidence of widespread under-age gambling. Some teenagers bet on card games and play on slot machines. Children are widely exposed to gambling ads, and many computer games mimic the experience of gambling as players compete to build up piles of virtual money.

GAMBLING IS ADDICTIVE

Some people find that once they start gambling, they just can't stop. Even though they know they're losing money, they keep on going, in the hope that their luck will change. Gamblers can easily get caught in a trap, where the more they lose, the more desperate they become to win their money back.

INVESTING

21

Some people decide to use a portion of their money for investing. This involves putting money into something that you believe will grow in value. Investments can bring rewards, but they can also be risky, and investors can lose the money they invested. Before investing money, people need to ask themselves:

- How much money can I afford to lose?
- Do I really need this money for something else?

DIFFERENT INVESTMENTS

People can choose to invest in a range of things. Some investors buy property and some buy art or classic cars, but the most common form of investment is to buy shares in a company or other organization.

BUYING SHARES

When investors buy shares in a company, they provide part of the money that's used to run that company. Companies are funded by millions of shares, so each share is a tiny part of the company's total wealth.

WHAT HAPPENS TO SHARES?

Shares can go up or down in value, depending on the success of the company.

- If a company does well, the value of its shares will rise. So, if investors sell their shares, they will make a profit.

↑ **PROFIT**

LOSS ↓

- If a company doesn't do as well as expected, the value of its shares will fall. So, if investors sell their shares, they will make a loss.

I bought 100 shares at $1 a share. The company has grown fast and now my shares are worth $3 each.

IF YOU SELL YOUR 100 SHARES NOW, YOU WILL BE PAID $300, AND MAKE A PROFIT OF $200 ON YOUR INVESTMENT.

I also bought 100 shares at $1 a share. The company hasn't done well and now my shares are worth 20 cents each.

IF YOU SELL YOUR 100 SHARES NOW, YOU WILL BE PAID $20, AND MAKE A LOSS OF $80 ON YOUR INVESTMENT.

163

PAYING DIVIDENDS

As well as making money from selling shares, shareholders may receive dividend payments from the company they've invested in. A dividend is a small share of a company's profit that is paid out to its shareholders. The size of the dividend depends on how successful the company has been in a year and how many shares a shareholder owns.

INVESTMENT CHOICES

Before people make the decision to invest their money, they need to ask themselves:

- How much can I afford to invest?
- How long can I manage without the money I've invested?
- Do I want to go for a high-risk investment, which could earn more money, but could also lose everything I've put in?
- Do I prefer a lower-risk investment, which probably won't make so much money, but is more likely to keep my money safe?

The world of investment is very complicated, so people often rely on experts to help them make their investment choices. Financial experts advise their clients on which companies to invest in, and on the best times to buy and sell shares.

22. INSURANCE

Sometimes, unexpected things can ruin your financial plans. You may damage your phone, lose your wallet, or crash your bike. And, further in the future, you may face a range of expensive problems. Imagine how you'd feel if your car broke down or your home was flooded, or if you had an accident and lost your job. Serious problems like these are hard enough to deal with on their own, without the added worry of finding the money to pay for them.

So, how do you take steps to protect your money and make sure that, if you have a problem, it doesn't end up costing you a fortune?

BE PREPARED

People can prepare themselves for unexpected costs in these ways.

- Keeping money in reserve for emergencies. Turn back to page 106 for advice on saving up money for an emergency fund.

- Taking out insurance. Read the rest of this chapter to find out more.

WHAT IS INSURANCE?

Insurance is a way to protect yourself from paying out lots of money if things go wrong. People make regular payments (either once a year or once a month) to an insurance company in return for an insurance policy. The policy provides a guarantee to pay most of the costs if certain problems occur. As soon as people start paying for their policy, they are protected and they have the right to claim money from their insurance company.

ALL KINDS OF INSURANCE

You can take out insurance on your home, your possessions, your car, and on many other aspects of your life. (Turn to page 174 to find out more.)

Some insurance policies are mandatory. It is against the law in almost every state to drive a vehicle that is uninsured, and you can't take out a mortgage on a property unless you have homeowners insurance.

GET PROTECTED

Even though some insurance isn't mandatory, you could be taking a risk if you don't protect yourself. If you were going overseas, it would be a serious mistake to try to cut your costs by not paying for travel insurance.

HOW DOES INSURANCE WORK?

When people take out an insurance policy, they make a payment, called a premium, which can be paid monthly or yearly. The cost of the premium depends on the size of the risk and the value of what's being insured.

I'm an inexperienced driver so my auto insurance premium is high.

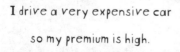

I've been driving for 20 years without any accidents so my premium is much lower than yours.

I drive a very expensive car so my premium is high.

My car would cost much less to repair than yours, so my premium is lower.

MAKING INSURANCE CLAIMS

When a problem occurs, policyholders submit a claim to the insurance company. The details of the claim are checked carefully before the insurance company agrees to pay out money.

Policyholders with a history of making lots of claims have to pay more for their insurance than people with fewer claims. People who haven't made any claims over a certain number of years are often rewarded by having money taken off the cost of their policy. This is called a "no claims discount."

OH NO! There goes my no claims discount!

CLUNK!

CRUNCH!

AUTO INSURANCE

In almost every state, if you own a vehicle, you have to buy auto insurance. This helps to cover the cost of accidents and other problems. There are three main types of insurance:

- Liability
  Covers the cost of damage to another person's vehicle or property if you are at fault.
- Collision
  Covers the same costs as liability insurance, with added financial coverage to repair your vehicle if it is also damaged.
- Comprehensive
  Covers all the costs described above, plus the cost of other types of damage to your vehicle. For example, if your car is stolen or vandalized.

The comprehensive policy is the most expensive, but if you choose one of the cheaper options, you risk facing some very large costs if something goes wrong.

HOMEOWNERS INSURANCE

All mortgage payers have to take out a homeowners insurance policy. This covers the cost of repairing a property if it is damaged in some way, for example, in a fire or a storm.

HOME CONTENTS INSURANCE

Home contents insurance covers the cost of replacing possessions that have been accidentally damaged or stolen. Clothes, computers, bicycles, and cell phones can all be included in a home contents insurance policy, even if they are lost or damaged outside the home.

TRAVEL INSURANCE

Travel insurance covers a range of expenses that travelers may face when they go on vacation or travel for work.

Most travel policies cover the cost of:

- Replacing lost or stolen bags and their contents.
- Expenses if flights are delayed or there are other travel problems.
- Having to cancel or cut short a vacation.
- Emergency medical expenses. (Your insurance policy will be more expensive if you're going on a high-risk vacation, such as a climbing or snowboarding trip.)

OTHER INSURANCE TYPES

It's possible to insure many different things, but here are some of the most common policies:

- Health insurance
  Covers some of the costs of medical treatment or care.
- Disability insurance
  Guarantees some income if the policyholder is unable to work.
- Loan protection
  Covers the costs of repaying a loan, if the borrower becomes unemployed.
- Life insurance
  Pays out money to family or other dependents if the policyholder dies.
- Pet insurance
  Covers the costs of some vets' bills.

FINDING HELP AND ADVICE

Now that you've read this book, you should be feeling confident about managing your money, but there may be times when you could use some advice.

If you're having problems, it's good to talk to someone you know well. There are also some useful websites offering clear advice on money management. Some of these sites have online helplines with trained advisors who can give personal support and advice. You'll find links to websites on Usborne Quicklinks, see page 4.

MONEY WORDS AND TERMS

allowance — regular money paid by parents or guardians to their children.

app — a software application that is designed to perform special functions and can be downloaded onto a phone, tablet, or other computer device.

APR — APR stands for Annual Percentage Rate. APR is used as a way of comparing different interest rates on loan repayments.

APY — APY stands for Annual Percentage Yield. APY is used as a way of comparing different interest rates on savings.

ATM — a machine that allows people to use their bankcards to take out cash and check their bank balance. ATM stands for Automated Teller Machine.

bank account — a service offered by a bank or credit union, allowing you to put money in, take money out, and pay bills, etc. The bank keeps a record of everything that happens to your money.

bank balance — the amount of money you have in your bank account.

bankcard — a plastic card issued by your bank or credit union that gives you access to the money in your account, either to withdraw or to spend. See also **debit card.**

bank loan — money that bank account holders arrange to borrow from their bank and then pay back, with an interest rate that has been arranged in advance.

budget — a way of planning your finances, in which you set out your income and expenses, then plan how to manage the rest of your money.

checking account — a bank account that is used to manage day-to-day money, for example, receiving wages and paying bills.

contract — a legal agreement between one person or organization and another person or organization, that says what both sides must do. For example, you could have a contract with a phone company or an internet service provider.

credit — money put into an account is "credited" to that account. If an account is "in credit," there is money in it that is available to spend. Another term for being in credit is "being in the black."

credit card — a plastic card available to over 18 year-olds that allows you to borrow money in order to make purchases. Credit cards have very high rates of interest on repayments.

credit score — a score given by a credit agency based on your history of borrowing and repayments. Your credit score reflects the level of risk involved in lending money to you. Another name for credit score is "credit rating."

credit union — an organization that is owned by its members, who have shares in the union. Credit unions offer the same services as banks.

cryptocurrency — virtual money that can be used online to buy and sell products and services.

currency — money used in a particular country, for example, dollars, pounds, and yen.

data — cellular data allows devices such as smartphones and tablets to access the internet when a Wi-Fi connection isn't available.

debit — money taken out of an account is "debited" from that account. If an account is "in debit," there is money owed on the account. Another term for being in debit is "being in the red."

debit card — a bankcard used to pay for things online or in a store without using cash. You can also use a debit card to withdraw money from your bank account, using an ATM.

debt — money you owe to another person or organization.

deduction — money taken off a salary, or wages, for income tax or other payments.

deposit — money paid into a bank account. See also **security deposit**.

direct debit — an instruction to a bank to release money from an account to make regular payments automatically. The billing company makes a direct request to the bank and can often change the amount requested.

discount — money taken off the price of something.

dividend — money from a company's profits paid to people who have shares in the company.

down payment — see **mortgage down payment.**

employee — someone who is paid to work for an organization, company, or individual.

employer — an organization, company, or individual who pays somebody else to work for them.

expenses — things you spend money on in order to live. Food and rent are examples of expenses.

Fairtrade — the Fairtrade movement aims to make sure that producers and workers are paid fairly for their work.

fixed interest rate — an interest rate that is guaranteed to stay the same for a fixed period of time.

fraud — the crime of deceiving people in some way, often to gain money.

gambling — risking money on a game or other activity at which you can win or lose.

gross income — the total pay that people receive before any deductions (such as income tax and health insurance) are made.

in-app charge — a charge for a purchase made inside an app.

income — money that you earn or receive. Your income is your "money in."

income tax — a tax that has to be paid to the government that is proportionate to the amount people earn.

installment plan — a way of paying for expensive items by borrowing the total cost and making regular repayments, plus interest.

insurance — a way to protect yourself from losing money if something goes wrong. You make a regular payment (known as a premium) to an insurance company in return for their guarantee of some financial protection. There are many different types of insurance, such as auto insurance, homeowners insurance, travel insurance, and disability insurance.

interest — money that is added to loan repayments or to savings in a bank account.

interest rate — a set percentage of a loan or of savings that determines how much interest is paid.

investing — using money to buy something that may increase in value over time, for example shares in a company.

leasing agent — someone who helps a landlord to find tenants, and organizes rent payments and repairs.

line of credit — an amount of money, which is made available to an individual by a bank or credit union, with interest added.

loan — a sum of money that you borrow from a bank, an organization, or an individual, usually with interest added.

loan shark — someone who lends money without obeying the laws on lending.

minimum repayment — the smallest possible amount that must be paid off each month on a credit card or store card debt.

minimum wage — the lowest hourly wage that employers are allowed to pay by law.

mortgage — a long-term loan from a credit union or bank that allows people to buy their own home. Mortgages are paid back over a number of years.

mortgage down payment — a sum of money that people must pay upfront towards the cost of a property when they are taking out a mortgage to buy it.

needs — things you cannot do without.

net income — the pay that people receive after deductions, such as income taxes, are made. Net income is sometimes called "take-home pay."

online banking — a method of managing your bank account from your smartphone, tablet, or computer. Online banking is sometimes called "internet banking."

overdrawn — a bank account is overdrawn if the balance of the account falls below zero. Banks usually charge high fees for being overdrawn unless you have a pre-arranged line of credit.

overtime — time worked in addition to the hours agreed with your employer, or the hours normally expected for the type of work you do.

payday lender — a lender who provides a short-term loan but charges extremely high rates of interest on the loan.

pension — regular payments made to people who have reached retirement age. There are several different types of pension plans, including private pensions and workplace pension plans, such as a 401-k. Also see **workplace pension plan.**

PIN — PIN stands for Personal Identification Number. This is a four-digit security number that is used with credit cards, bankcards, and online banking.

prepaid bankcard — a bankcard with money paid onto it in advance. Prepaid cards can be used for spending and withdrawing money.

profit — the amount of money left over after subtracting all costs and expenses.

receipt — a document given by a seller to a buyer as proof of a purchase. Receipts may be in paper or electronic form.

recurring payment — an instruction to a bank to release money from an account to make payments automatically. Only the account holder can change the payments.

rent — money paid by a tenant to the owner of a property (such as a house or an apartment).

retirement savings see **workplace pension plan.**

salary — a regular payment made by an employer to an employee. Salaries may be paid weekly, biweekly, or monthly.

savings account — a bank account designed for saving money. The bank pays you interest on your savings.

security deposit — money paid by a tenant before moving into a rented property as a way of protecting a landlord from the cost of any damage caused by that tenant.

shares — companies can be funded by millions of shares. Each share is a tiny part of the company's wealth. Shares can be paid for by investors, known as shareholders.

smartphone — a touch-screen phone that can access the internet.

statement — a document from your bank that shows all your recent financial activity.

store card — a card issued by a store or a chain of stores that works like a credit card. Store cards usually have even higher interest rates on repayments than credit cards.

store credit — a card or note issued by a store when a purchase is returned, allowing the customer to make an alternative purchase.

student loans — money borrowed by college students to cover the cost of their education.

subscription — a regular payment for a product, such as a mobile app or a magazine, or for a service, such as membership of a club. Subscriptions are often paid monthly.

subsidized loan — a student loan that does not usually gain interest while the student is studying.

tablet — a small, portable computer with a touch screen.

tap and go — a way of making a payment by waving or tapping a contactless device (such as a bankcard or a smartphone) on, or near, a machine reader.

tax — money paid to federal, state, or local governments. There are various taxes, including income tax and auto tax.

tenant — someone who lives in a property rented from a landlord.

unit price — the price for one item or unit of measurement (such as one pound or one gallon), that can be used to compare the same types of goods sold in varying packages.

unsubsidized loan — a student loan that usually starts to gain interest as soon as the loan is made available to the student.

variable interest rate — an interest rate on repayments that is not fixed, so the size of the interest payments may change.

wage — a payment for hours worked, using a set hourly rate. Wages are usually paid either biweekly or weekly.

wants — things you would like to buy, but you could do without. See also **needs.**

Wi-Fi — a wireless connection to an internet router, which provides internet to homes and businesses. Wi-Fi connections are only available close to the router.

withdrawal — money taken out of a bank or credit union account.

workplace pension plan — a retirement savings plan set up by an employer for their employees. A percentage of an employee's salary is paid into an investment fund and matched in some way by their employer. The most common workplace pension plan is a 401-k.

QUIZ ANSWERS

page 30

> <u>Wants</u>: bubblegum, movie ticket, lipstick, magazine, perfume, candy.
>
> <u>Needs</u>: banana, bus ticket, deodorant, sandwiches, socks, toothpaste.

page 52

> a) Materials cost per puppet = $2.50
> b) Labor cost per puppet = $2
> c) Total cost per puppet = $4.50
> d) You should charge $6 for each puppet.

page 67

> The best deals are:
> a) 2 for 1, c) 2/3 original price, f) 60% off
> The new discounted prices are: Shorts: $15, T-shirt: $8

page 108

> a) You would have $30 to spend on presents.
> b) You should set aside $10 each week.
> c) You will reach your savings target in 8 months.

INDEX

A

Allowances, 24–26

Apprenticeships, 124

Apps, 79–81

APR, 120, 150, 154

APY, 120

ATMs, 16, 115–117

Auctions (online), 70

Auto insurance, 169–171

B

Bank accounts, 15, 87, 107, 110–123, 148

    Balances, 116, 121

    Checking accounts, 110–117, 148

    Deposits, 112

    Direct debits, 139–141

    Education accounts, 120

    Joint checking accounts, 111–117

Online banking, 113, 121–123

Recurring payments, 141

Savings accounts, 107, 110–111, 119–120

Withdrawals, 112, 117

Youth savings accounts, 111, 119–120

Bankcards, 16, 80–81, 87, 113–118

Cancelling your card, 117

Lost cards, 117

PIN (Personal Identification Number), 115–116

Prepaid cards, 80, 118

Banks, 15, 107, 110–123, 140–141, 144, 147–151

Online-only banks, 111

Bargains, 56, 63–64, 68

Bills (to pay), 110, 138–141, 146

Bitcoin, 19

Borrowing money, 147–158

Budgets, 34–39, 95, 104–106

Budgeting for gifts, 95

Budgeting for saving, 104–106

Emergency funds, 106, 167

Household budgets, 39, 146

Buying a home, 142, 144–145

Buying online, 16, 64, 68–71, 82–87

C

Charities, 96–99, 141

Sponsorship, 97–99

Checks, 15

Checking accounts, 110–117, 148

Coupons, 56, 91–92

Credit cards, 147, 150, 152–155

Credit scores, 155, 158

Credit unions, 111, 144

D

Data (for phones), 74–77

Debit cards, 113–117

Debt, 153, 156–157

Direct debits, 139–141

Disability insurance, 174

Discounts, 53, 57–59, 91, 137

Dividends, 164

E

Expenses, 34–37, 104–105, 146

F

Fairtrade, 96

Federal Work-Study Program, 136

Fees, 81, 117, 136, 143, 148, 155, 158

   Borrowing fees, 148, 155, 158

   Cancellation fees, 81

   College fees, 136

   Rental fees, 143

   Subscription fees, 81

Fraud, 123

Free trials, 81

Full-time jobs, 125–129

G
Gambling, 159–160
Gaming, 78–79
  Apps, 79
  Free trials, 81
  In-app charges, 80
  Subscriptions, 81
Gifts, 27, 93–95, 100
Grants, 136

H
Health insurance, 130–131, 174
Homes, 142–146
  Bills, 138–141, 146
  Buying a home, 142, 144–145
  Insurance, 146, 168, 172
  Mortgages, 142, 144–145, 155, 168

Renting, 142–144

I

In-app charges, 80

Income, 22, 31, 34–38, 104–105, 174

Income tax, 126, 130–131

Installment plans, 151

Insurance, 73, 166–174

  Auto insurance, 169–171

  Disability insurance, 174

  Health insurance, 130–131, 174

  Homeowners insurance, 146, 168, 172

  Home contents insurance, 73, 172

  Insurance claims, 170

  Insurance premiums, 169

  No claims discount, 170

  Travel insurance, 168, 173

Interest, 110, 119–120, 148–156

  APR, 120, 150, 154

APY, 120

Fixed interest rate, 154

Interest on borrowing, 144–145, 148–156

Interest on savings, 110, 119–120

Variable interest rate, 154

Investments, 161–165

Dividends, 164

Shares, 161–165

J

Jobs, 40–46, 124–129, 137

Full-time, 125–129

Part-time, 40–46, 124–129, 137

Seasonal, 127

Joint checking accounts, 111–117

L

Leasing agents, 143

Line of credit, 147–148

Loan sharks, 156

Loans, 120, 133–135, 147–158

  APR, 120, 150, 154

  Bank loans, 147, 150–151

  Credit cards, 147, 150, 152–155

  Credit scores, 155, 158

  Installment plans, 151

  Interest on borrowing, 144–145, 148–156

  Mortgages, 142, 144–145, 155

  Payday loans, 156

  Store cards, 150, 153–154

  Student loans, 133–135

  Subsidized loans, 134

  Unsubsidized loans, 134

M

Minimum wage, 126

Mortgages, 142, 144–145, 155

  Down payments, 145

O

Online banking, 113, 121–123

Overdrawn (being), 148

Overtime, 128

P

Part-time jobs, 40–46, 124–129, 137

Pay, 124–132

  Pay stubs, 130

Pensions, 130, 132

Phones, 72–77, 166, 172

  Apps, 79–81

  BYOP plans, 76

  Contracts, 74–77

  Data use, 74–77

Prepaid cards, 80, 118

Profit, 48–51

Proof of purchase, 84–87

Q

Quizzes, 10–11, 30, 52, 67, 108–109

R

Receipts, 23, 54, 84–87

  E-receipts, 84

Recurring payments, 141

Refunds, 54, 82–87

    Proof of purchase, 84–87

    Store credit, 84–85

Renting, 142–144

  Landlords, 144

  Leasing agents, 143

  Security deposits, 143–144

Retirement savings plans, 130, 132

Returns, 54, 69, 82–87

  Return policy, 69, 83–87

  Time limits, 84, 86

S

Salaries, 125–132

Sales, 63, 83

Savings, 38–39, 100–107, 111, 119–120

   Savings accounts, 107, 110-111, 119–120

   Savings plan, 102–105

Scholarships, 136

Second-hand stores, 64

Selling online, 68, 71

Shares, 161–165

Special offers, 53, 57, 63, 153

Sponsorship, 97–99

Store cards, 150, 153–154

Store credit, 84–85

Student discounts, 137

Student loans, 133–135

Subscriptions, 81, 141

Subsidized loans, 134

T

Taxes, 126, 130–131

Terms and conditions, 86, 91, 111

Thrift stores, 64, 97

Travel insurance, 168, 173

U

Unit price, 60–61

Unsubsidized loans, 134

W

Wages, 124–132

  Minimum wage, 126

Y

Youth savings accounts, 111, 119–120

Additional editing by
Jessica Greenwell and Hannah Watson

With additional design by Tilly Kitching

Usborne Publishing Ltd., Usborne House, 83-85 Saffron Hill,
London EC1N 8RT, England. www.usborne.com
Printed in China. Copyright ©2019 Usborne Publishing Ltd.
First published in America in 2019. AE.

When using the internet, please follow the internet safety guidelines shown
at the Usborne Quicklinks website. The links at Usborne Quicklinks are
regularly reviewed and updated, but Usborne Publishing is not repsonsible and
does not accept liability for the content of any website other than its own.
We recommend that all children are supervised while using the internet.